TALES OF WISD[OM]

Inspiring Stories for Young Hearts

Includes lessons, new words, puzzles, activities, etc.

Written by:
Kafeelah Adenekan

TALES OF WISDOM:
Inspiring Stories for Young Hearts
INCLUDES LESSONS, NEW WORDS, PUZZLES, ACTIVITIES, ETC.

PUBLISHED IN ENGLAND BY

TRANQUILITY HUB LTD

© TRANQUILITY HUB LTD 2023

WEBSITE: WWW.TRANQUILITYHUB.COM

ALL RIGHTS RESERVED.

ISBN 978-1-914286-10-0 PAPERBACK

THIS STORY BOOK BELONGS TO:

_____

INTRODUCTION:

بِسْمِ اللَّهِ الرَّحْمَنِ الرَّحِيمِ

Welcome to "Tales of Wisdom: Inspiring Stories for Young Hearts"! This special book is made just for you, filled with enchanting stories that have important lessons to teach us. These stories are about being kind, brave, honest, and making good choices.

In these pages, you will find stories that teach us about kindness, helping others, and being grateful. But we will also learn about things we should be careful of, like being greedy, telling lies, and being stubborn. These stories remind us that our actions have consequences, and it's important to choose wisely.

Each story in this book has a special message for you. They will inspire you and help you on your own journey. You will learn about empathy, forgiveness, and the importance of standing up for what's right. You will also meet brave and wise characters who will capture your imagination and teach you valuable lessons.

Parents, guardians, and teachers can join you in reading these stories and discussing the lessons together. You can learn and grow together with the wisdom from these tales.

Are you ready to begin this amazing adventure? Open your heart, turn the page, and let the magic of these stories fill your imagination. Get ready to be inspired, learn new things, and have lots of fun.

Enjoy reading "Tales of Wisdom: Inspiring Stories for Young Hearts"!

Happy reading!

TABLE OF CONTENT

- Introduction

- Kindness and Compassion
Story One: What A Man!
Story Two: Neighbours' Right

- Lessons Learned the Hard Way
Story Three: It Is No Joke
Story Four: The Stubborn Boy
Story Five: The Greedy Boy

- Generosity and Trust in Allah
Story Six: Allah the Bountiful
Story Seven: Where is Your Proof?

- Consequences of Actions
Story Eight: Equality and Justice
Story Nine: The Three Young Men

KINDNESS AND COMPASSION

WHAT A MAN!

Once upon a time, in the city of Makkah, there lived a truly remarkable man. Everyone knew him for his kindness, wisdom, and strong belief in the truth. He always told people to worship only one God and to be good to one another.

Unfortunately, there were some bad people in Makkah who worshipped idols and did bad things.

They did not like the message of this man, and they caused him and his followers a lot of pain and suffering.

They would make fun of him, say mean things and even throw dirt at him. One lady, in particular, would throw garbage at him or in his path whenever he walked by her house.

This honest and trustworthy man never gave up. He kept spreading his message of truth; reminding people of the importance of worshipping one God and doing good deeds.

Even though he faced many challenges, he never stopped being kind and compassionate.

One day, as the good man walked by the lady's house, something different happened. She didn't throw any dirt at him. He became curious and asked about her.

He found out that she was sick and resting at home. So, he decided to visit her and see how she was doing. He offered to help her with chores around the house to make her life easier during her sickness.

The old woman was shocked and humbled by his kindness. She felt embarrassed about how she had treated him before. She said, "Even though I did bad things to you, you still care about me?

This shows that what you have brought is the truth." And in that moment, she accepted the good man's message.

This remarkable man was **Prophet Muhammad** ﷺ, and his message is **Islam**.

His actions left a lasting impression on the people who met him.

He showed them that it's possible to respond to mean behaviour with good, to heal wounds with forgiveness, and to make the world a better place through acts of kindness and compassion.

His teachings continue to inspire people to this day.

Fun Fact:

Did you know that Prophet Muhammad ﷺ, the good man in the story is considered one of the most influential people in history?

His teachings and message of peace, unity, and compassion have inspired billions of people around the world for centuries.

He is the last and final prophet of Allah and his words continue to guide and uplift hearts to this day.

Learn more about this remarkable man as you journey through life.

LESSONS

1 KINDNESS

The remarkable man in the story showed kindness to everyone, even those who were mean to him. He visited the old woman who had been throwing garbage at him and helped her when she was sick.

2 TRUTH

The good man believed in the importance of telling the truth and worshipping only one God.

3 HELPING OTHERS

The good man taught us to help people who are in need, like the sick old woman.

4 FORGIVENESS

Even when people were mean to him, the good man forgave them and showed them love and compassion.

New Words

Worship: To worship means to show respect and love for God.

Remarkable: worthy of attention; striking.

City: A city is a large and busy place where many people live and work.

Worship: To worship means to show respect and love for God.

Wisdom: Wisdom means having knowledge and good judgment to make wise decisions.

Humbled: When someone is humbled, it means they feel modest or humble, realizing their own weaknesses.

Idol: An idol is an object that people worship as a god.

Uplift: To uplift means to make someone feel better or to improve a situation.

QUESTIONS

01. What did the remarkable man teach people to do?

02. How did the bad people in Makkah treat the good man?

03. What did the old woman do when the good man passed by her house?

04. How did the good man respond to the old woman's actions?

05. What lessons can we learn from the story?

06. Why is it important to be kind to others, even if they are mean to us?

07. How did the good man's actions inspire the old woman to change?

08. What is the name of the remarkable man in the story and what was his message called?

REMINDER

"It's important to be kind, truthful, and forgiving, just like the good man in the story. Helping others when they need it is also a wonderful thing to do.!

★ ★ ★ ★ ★

NEIGHBOURS' RIGHT

A long time ago, there lived a man named Sheikh Mahmud. He was known for his piety and kindness.

Sheikh Mahmud always treated others with respect, cared for the elderly, and showed kindness to the young. He lived in a small house with a fence that separated him from his neighbour.

His neighbour's toilet had a pipe which passed under the fence into Sheikh Mahmud's house and out into the central sewage.

Unfortunately, the pipe was faulty and dripped waste into Sheikh Mahmud's compound.

Despite this inconvenience, Sheikh Mahmud didn't want to hurt his neighbour's feelings or cause any trouble. He knew his neighbour was poor and couldn't afford to repair or replace the pipe.

Every day for ten years, Sheikh Mahmud collected

the waste in a bucket and disposed of it himself, keeping his house clean and maintaining peace with his neighbour.

One day, Sheikh Mahmud fell seriously ill and felt that his end was near. He called his neighbour and said:

"Dear neighbour, I am very sick and fear that I may not have much time left. For ten years, I have endured the dripping waste from your toilet in my house, silently disposing of it so as not to quarrel with you but if I pass away, I worry that the person who will live here after me may not be as patient. I kindly request you to repair the pipe and spare your future neighbour from this trouble."

His neighbour was shocked and said "so you have been enduring me for the past ten years! You are a good man and an excellent example for those who wish to live in peace with others.

I will repair the pipe as you have said and will emulate you till I die. Henceforth, I have embraced your religion and way of life."

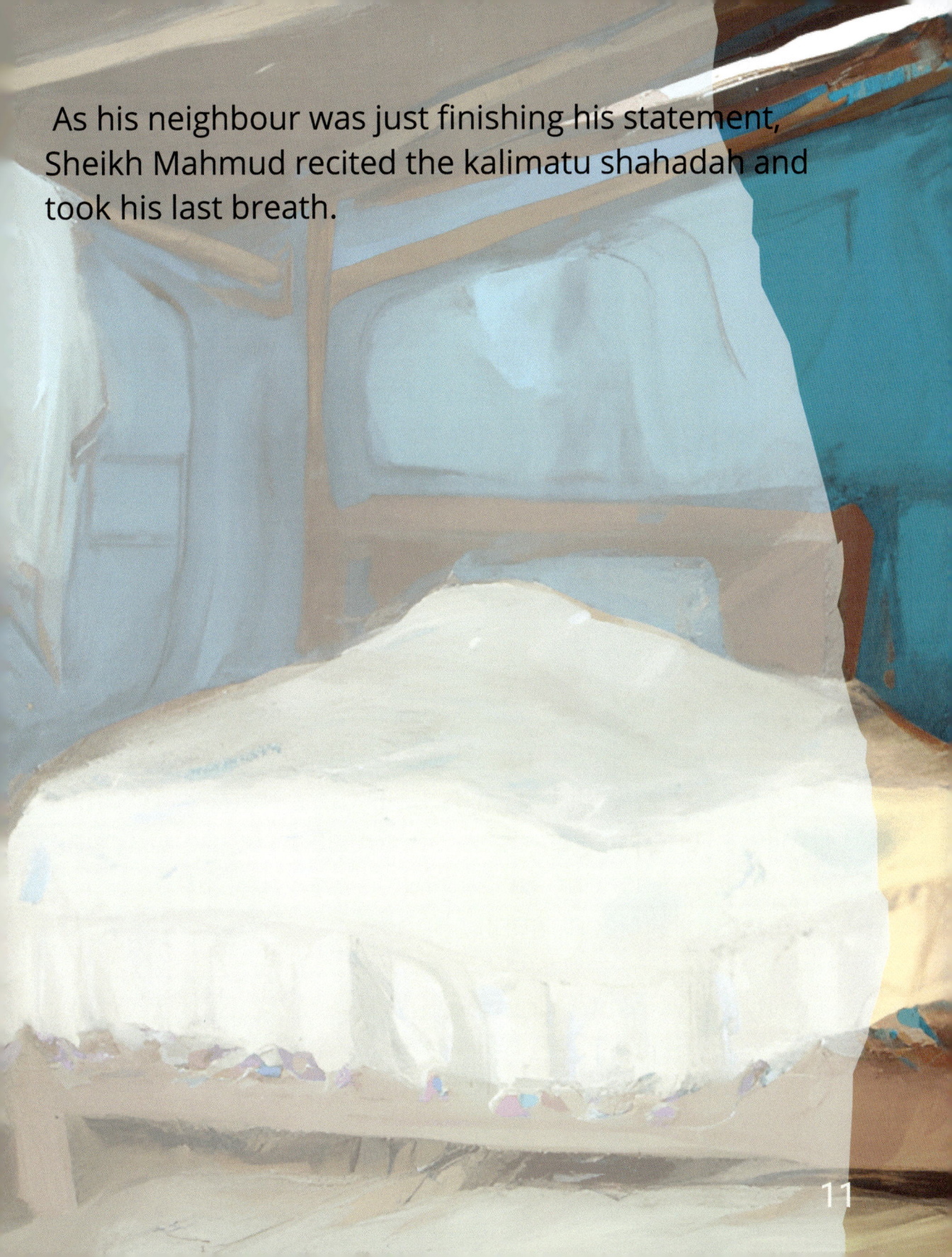

As his neighbour was just finishing his statement, Sheikh Mahmud recited the kalimatu shahadah and took his last breath.

Fun Fact:

The heart-warming tale "Neighbours' Right" is deeply rooted in the teachings of Prophet Muhammad ﷺ.

In Islam, the rights of neighbours are highly regarded and emphasized. Prophet Muhammad ﷺ provided profound guidance on treating neighbours with kindness and respect.

One of the famous hadiths (sayings) of Prophet Muhammad ﷺ, regarding the rights of neighbours is: "Jibreel (Gabriel) kept advising me about the neighbour until I thought that he would make an heir (of one's neighbour)."

This hadith highlights the importance of treating neighbours so well that it is as if they are part of one's family. It encourages us to be considerate, helpful, and caring towards our neighbours, fostering strong and compassionate community bonds.

Let this tale inspire you to embody the spirit of Prophet Muhammad's ﷺ teachings, nurturing positive relationships with your neighbours and spreading love and unity within your community.

LESSONS

1 We should strive to live in peace and harmony with others, even in challenging situations.

2 Tolerance is an important virtue that allows us to coexist peacefully with our neighbours.

3 Our actions and character can influence others positively and teach them to be good.

New Words

Unintentional: Not done on purpose or without the intention of causing harm.

Emulate: To copy or follow as an example.

Tolerate: To allow something to happen without getting upset or angry.

Uplift: To uplift means to make someone feel better or to improve a situation.

Dispose: get rid of by throwing away or giving or selling to someone else.

QUESTIONS

01. What was the name of the pious man in the story?

02. What was the problem with the pipe from his neighbour's toilet?

03. Is it good to engage in quarrels with our neighbours?

REMINDER

"Respect and kindness towards our neighbors are essential. Always be considerate and willing to help, even in small ways. Treat others as you would like to be treated and build strong, positive relationships."

★★★★★

KINDNESS AND COMPASSION NEW WORDS PUZZLE

Words can be found in any direction (including diagonals) and can overlap each other. Use the word bank below.

```
C H L B Z F E K A L I M A T U O V F S E
Q I G Z E E M B A R R A S S E D M K K E
D W P C H T X H Z Y N O I T A R I M D A
U I C S X S R C C Y N C G F B R H J Z V
N S J Y K F Q I S C L D X S X Y I U D Q
I D U A C E Y E I S U W K D T V A D Y A
N O U P R J M J L B O E L I V L I N O I
T M P D L U Y A O R N I T S X N U Z O L
E B I X L I G I S U Q A P Z D X X S D X
N G J A D R F H I T U T H E P B R H N G
T U T S I G I T G P T U L F P M E S S I
I E L X S P C T U G M I M Y B D S L H T
O A U K P G F T C B B U Z R R K I K A B
N N C W O C J D L L M M N A E C L I H Z
A J L M S G A E E M K K X Q I V I R A J
L S T W E N D B N A T Q Y T W I E Y D N
T Q P Y B R M K Z Q Q N Y R M Y N N A G
L E L B A K R A M E R U T G P G C X H E
S J L W F R D W X K R P J W S N E O N Z
V Y N U Y V D G P Z R L T O L E R A T E
```

Word Bank

1. WORSHIP
2. KALIMATU
3. IDOL
4. WISDOM
5. CITY
6. UPLIFT
7. SHAHADAH
8. HUMBLED
9. UNINTENTIONAL
10. INDELIBLE
11. INSULTS
12. EMULATE
13. ADMIRATION
14. EMBARRASSED
15. TOLERATE
16. RESILIENCE
17. DISPOSE
18. REMARKABLE

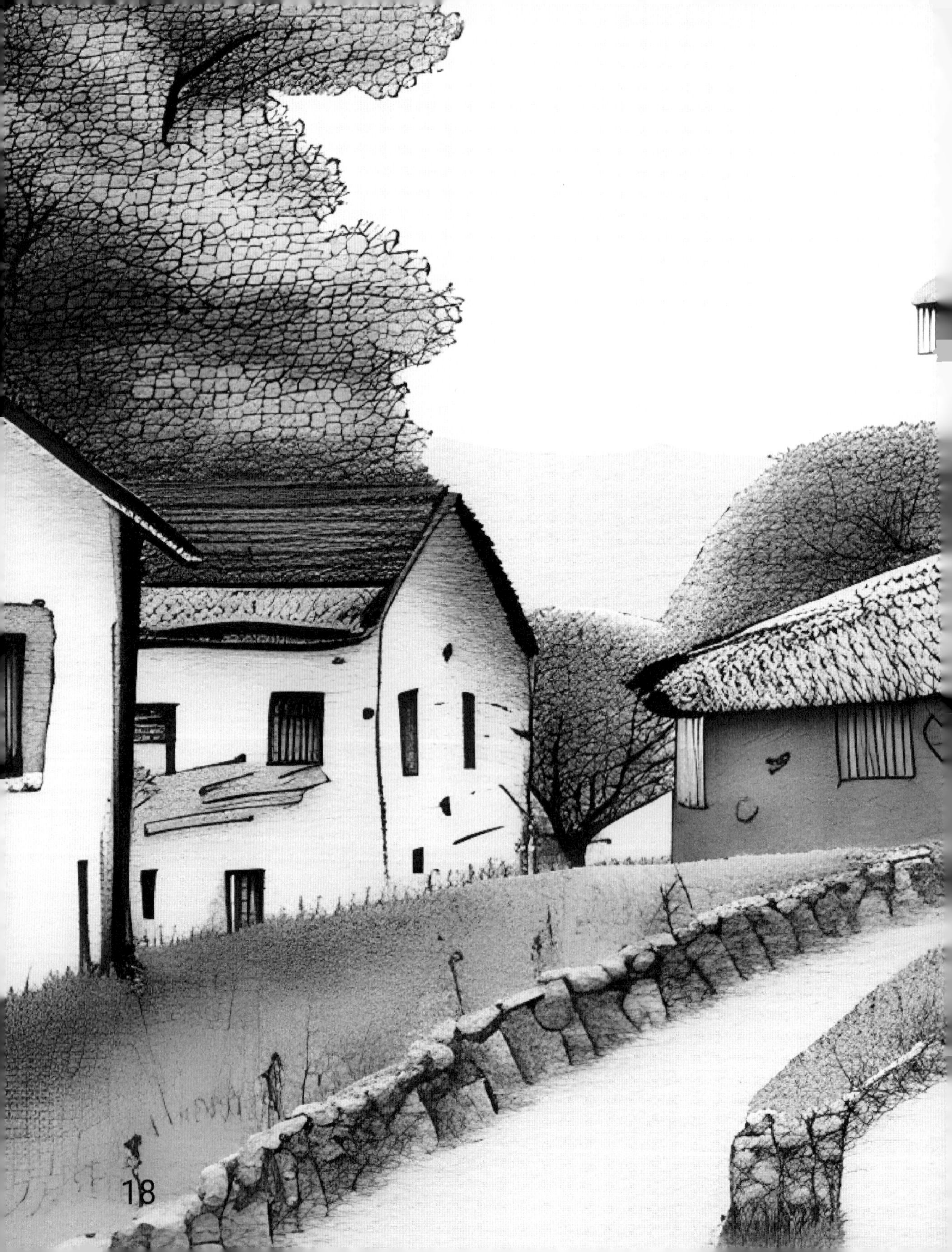

LEARNING THE HARD WAY

It Is No Joke

Once upon a time, in a faraway village, there was a man named Kijo. Kijo had a habit of telling jokes and making people laugh. But sometimes, he would take his jokes too far and tell lies just to get a reaction from others.

One sunny day, while Kijo was on his farm, he decided to play a trick on the villagers. He started shouting for help, pretending that something bad had happened. Worried, the villagers rushed to his aid, only to find Kijo laughing and saying, "Sorry, it was just a joke!"

Some people felt upset because they thought something terrible had really happened while others just laughed, and they all went away.

Another day, Kijo was in his house when he yelled, "Fire! Fire! Help me, I'm burning!" Concerned neighbours quickly ran to his house, afraid that he was in danger.

When they arrived, they saw that there was no fire at all. Kijo was laughing and said, "April fools! It was only a prank." This time, the villagers didn't find it funny. They felt annoyed and decided not to take Kijo seriously anymore.

One night, the villagers heard Kijo cry for help again. They thought he was just joking as usual, so nobody went to help him The next morning, people woke up to see
Kijo's house completely burnt and his corpse lying on the floor.

If not because they were sure it was his house, they would not have recognized him because the fire had consumed him beyond recognition.

'Oh, poor kijo! If he had not always joked with lies, he would not have died this way!' One man lamented.

The villagers realized a very important lesson from this sad event; **it is crucial to never joke with lies**.

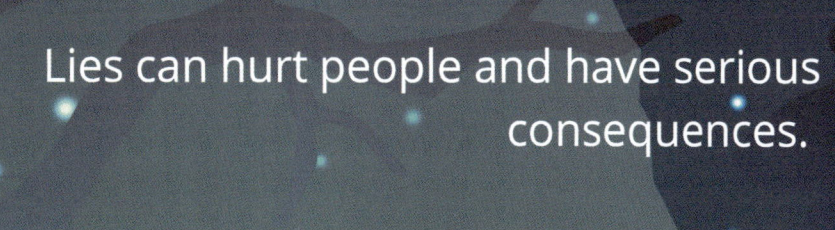

Lies can hurt people and have serious consequences.

Kijo's constant joking had made others stop taking him seriously, even when he really needed help.

If only Kijo had not joked with lies, things might have turned out differently.

Fun Fact:

The story "It Is No Joke" reminds us of the importance of honesty and the consequences of playful deception. In various cultures and traditions, the value of truthfulness is upheld as a pillar of strong character.

One of the hadiths (sayings) of Prophet Muhammad ﷺ that emphasizes the significance of honesty is:

""I enjoin you to be truthful, for truthfulness leads to righteousness and righteousness leads to Paradise. A man may continue to tell the truth and endeavour to be truthful until he is recorded with Allah as a speaker of truth. And beware of lying, for lying leads to wickedness and wickedness leads to Hell. A man may continue to tell lies and endeavour to tell lies until he is recorded with Allah as a liar."
[Muslim, 2607]

This hadith highlights the direct link between honesty and goodness, with the path of truthfulness leading to the ultimate reward of Paradise. It serves as a gentle reminder of the blessings that honesty brings into our lives.

As you enjoy "It Is No Joke," take a moment to reflect on the timeless wisdom shared by Prophet Muhammad ﷺ.

Let this delightful tale inspire you to be truthful and sincere in all your actions, fostering a life of integrity and righteousness.

LESSONS

1 Honesty:
Honesty is important. It's crucial to be truthful and not joke with lies.

2 Tolerance:
Tolerance is an important virtue that allows us to coexist peacefully with our neighbours.

3 Good Character
Our actions and character can influence others positively and teach them to be good.

New Words

Recognition: Recognition: The ability to know or identify something.

Villagers: People who live in a village

Consumed: When something is completely destroyed or devoured.

Consequences: The results or effects of actions.

Corpse: The lifeless body of a person or animal.

Hurriedly: Doing something quickly and in a rush.

Suddenly: When something happens quickly and unexpectedly.

QUESTIONS

01. What is the name of the man mentioned in the passage?

02. What was bad about his habit?

03. Why did some people get upset with Kijo's jokes?

04. What happened to Kijo's house?

05. Why is it important to be honest?

06. How can we show respect to others when it comes to joking and pranks?

07. Is pranking with April fools a good idea?

REMINDER

"Honesty is key! Telling the truth and not playing jokes with lies can prevent harm and maintain trust. Think before you act and consider how your words and actions may affect others."

★★★★★

The Stubborn Boy

There once was a little boy named Ali. Ali was very stubborn. He never liked to listen to instructions or be corrected when he made mistakes.

Whenever Ali went to someone's house, he would simply enter without knocking or asking for permission. People would often complain to Ali's mother about his behaviour.

His mother would warn him, saying, "Always seek permission before entering someone's house. Don't you know that Allah and His messenger ﷺ have advised us against entering people's houses without permission?"

However, Ali paid no attention.

One day, Ali's mother sent him to visit one of her friends. When Ali arrived at the friend's house, he didn't bother to knock or ask for permission before entering.

This behaviour annoyed his mother's friend, and she reported Ali to his mother.

His mother punished him for his actions, but Ali would not listen. He refused to listen to instructions and said, "After all, the door was made for everyone to enter through."

On another day, Ali went to visit his friend Jaafar. As usual, Ali opened the door to the house without knocking.

Unfortunately, just as Ali was about to enter, Jaafar's mother opened the door and accidentally poured a bucket of used hot water on Ali.

Ouch!

Ali suffered serious burns and had to stay in the hospital for more than two months.

From that day on, Ali never forgot to knock and ask for permission before entering someone's house. He even started knocking on the door of his own room occasionally. He had learned his lesson the hard way.

FUN FACT:

In the story "The Stubborn Boy," the character's journey of learning to listen and compromise reflects a valuable lesson found in various cultures and traditions.

One of the hadiths (sayings) of Prophet Muhammad ﷺ states, "I guarantee a house in the surroundings of Paradise for a man who avoids quarrelling even if he were in the right, a house in the middle of Paradise for a man who avoids lying even if he were joking, and a house in the upper part of Paradise for a man who made his character good."
Sunan Abu Dawood (4883)

This hadith emphasizes the strength of character and self-control exhibited by those who can remain patient and avoid stubbornness in the face of challenges or disagreements.

It teaches the importance of being open to compromise and finding solutions through calmness and understanding.

"The Stubborn Boy" offers a narrative of personal growth and the rewards of embracing patience and flexibility. As you delve into this wonderful tale, remember the timeless wisdom found in the hadith and let it inspire you to cultivate a patient and adaptable spirit, fostering harmonious relationships with those around you.

LESSONS

1 It is important to always knock and seek permission before entering someone's house.

2 Listen to instructions and advice, especially from our parents.

3 Refrain from doing anything that Allah (The Exalted) and His prophet (peace be upon him) have forbidden.

New Words

Stubborn: Not wanting to change or be flexible.

Instruction: Guidance or directions given to teach or inform.

Mistakenly: Doing something foolishly or in error.

Permission: Approval or consent to do something.

Hospitalized: Admitted and kept in the hospital for treatment.

Determined: Having a strong resolve or intention to do something without changing.

Unfortunately: Unluckily or regrettably.

QUESTIONS

01. Ali was a _____ boy.

02. What was the name of Ali's friend?

03. Who forbids us from entering other people's houses without permission?

04. Who accidentally threw hot water on Ali?

05. Do you think Ali is a good boy?

REMINDER

"Listen and learn from others. Being stubborn can lead to missed opportunities and misunderstandings. Embrace humility, be open to guidance, and understand the importance of following instructions."

★★★★★

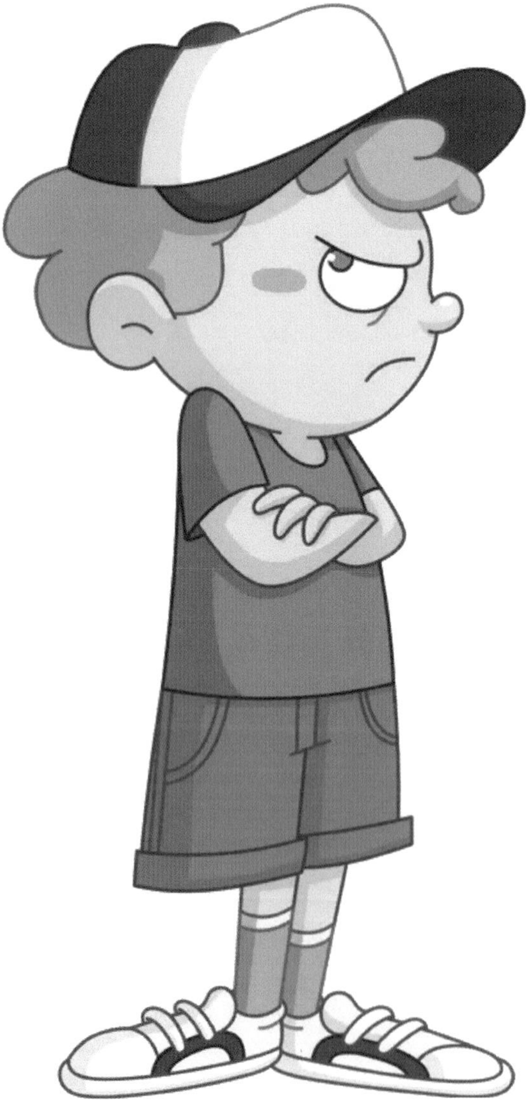

The Greedy Boy

Once upon a time, there was a boy named Umar. He was very greedy and was never satisfied with what he had.

Whenever someone gave him something, whether it was his mother or anyone else, he would complain that others had received more. Even when he ate with others, he would rush through his meal, always wanting to eat more than his fair share.

One evening, Umar sat down to have dinner with his brothers. He quickly noticed that the piece of meat on his elder brother's side of the plate was bigger than the one in front of him. Umar became fixated on having the larger piece of meat. An idea crossed his mind. He pretended to be drinking water and he cunningly used the water in the cup to extinguish the burning lamp.

As the room fell into darkness, everyone was confused and began searching for matches to relight the lamp.

Umar joined in the search, pretending to look for matches. In the darkness, he dipped his hand into the plate and grabbed the bigger piece of meat. Greedily, he put it into his mouth and started chewing.

Soon after, his elder brother found the matches and lit the lamp. Umar saw his brother's meat still in the plate and took a closer look at what he was eating.

Noooo!

He screamed in horror.

He had unknowingly eaten a cockroach that had landed in the food when the light went out.

Poor Umar! He vomited uncontrollably, emptying his stomach of all the food he had consumed.

The experience of eating the meat with the cockroach shocked him deeply, and he made a promise to himself never to be greedy again.

FUN FACT:

In the thought-provoking story "The Greedy Boy," the consequences of greed serve as a cautionary tale that echoes universal themes found in various cultures and belief systems.

One of the hadiths (sayings) of Prophet Muhammad (Peace and blessings of Allah be upon him) that touches on the dangers of greed is:

"Beware of greed, for it was only greed that destroyed those before you. It commanded them to be miserly and they did so. It commanded them to severe family ties and they did so. It commanded them to behave wickedly and they did so."

This hadith warns against the allure of greed, reminding us to be content with what we have and avoid excessive desires for material possessions. It encourages gratitude for the provisions we are granted and emphasizes the virtue of moderation.

"The Greedy Boy" exemplifies the importance of cultivating a balanced and grateful outlook in life. As you immerse yourself in this captivating tale, ponder the timeless wisdom of the hadith and let it inspire you to nurture a generous spirit, free from the pitfalls of greed. Embrace contentment and gratitude, and discover the joy in appreciating life's simple blessings.

LESSONS

1 It is important to be content and satisfied with what we have.

2 We should learn to share with others, even if it means taking a smaller portion.

New Words

- **Idea:** A thought or plan.
- **Satisfied:** The feeling of being content and accepting what one has.
- **Dinner:** The last meal of the day.
- **Struck:** To hit or come to mind suddenly.
- **Noticed:** To observe or pay attention to something.
- **Cunningly:** In a clever and deceitful way.
- **Scream:** A loud cry or shout, quickly and unexpectedly.
- **Pretended:** To act as if something is true or behave in a certain way.

QUESTIONS

01. What is the name of the greedy boy?

02. Is it good to be greedy?

03. Would you like to be like Umar? Why or why not?

REMINDER

"Practice gratitude and contentment. Greed can never bring lasting happiness. Appreciate what you have, and share with others. Learn the joy of giving and the value of being satisfied with what you possess."

★★★★★

LEARNING THE HARD WAY NEW WORDS PUZZLE

Words can be found in any direction (including diagonals) and can overlap each other. Use the word bank below.

```
B O K A N I V X C S R N H Y S R G K U H
N A D D O W Y P O T J X S X A N P N C D
O M H E I R B D N R F X N F V Y F D O C
I I H T S E L P S U J X G E L O S N N J
T S I E S C S H U C H V T H R R R S F
C T W R I O C X M K D J S T E T Z I I B
U A F M M G L W E Y Q I U G J T G Y D H
R K F I R N G T D N L N A K Y D F X E O
T E P N E I F K B Y A L J I W S R J R S
S N F E P T Y R T T L G O M U H U F A P
N L E D Q I W S E I B E K I I S Q D T I
I Y G K Q O L L V K A B F J T Y F E E T
V P D Q B N Y H L W Y S M U Q L D D N A
H U R R I E D L Y A H R B X E N N T L
J O H K O D X O R Y M B R I Q E E E D I
U I W V P U P A I T O E P A F D S T Y Z
A V D V C X P Z B R K L N Q M D P E R E
V C G E B M J V N J J A T T U U R R J D
V Q K L A E Y O Y C I K E V E S O P O H
S E C N E U Q E S N O C Y D X D C U E M
```

WORD BANK

1. PRETENDED
2. UNFORTUNATELY
3. LAMENTED
4. HURRIEDLY
5. CONSUMED
6. CORPSE
7. IDEA
8. PERMISSION
9. RECOGNITION
10. STRUCK
11. MISTAKENLY
12. VILLAGERS
13. SUDDENLY
14. STUBBORN
15. STYLISHLY
16. CONSEQUENCES
17. DETERMINED
18. CONSIDERATE
19. HOSPITALIZED
20. INSTRUCTION

44

Generosity and Trust in Allah

Allah the Bountiful

A long time ago in a far way land, lived a poor man named Fadl. He was very poor and wanted to be rich. Fadl approached a pious man and said, "Oh, pious man! Please pray to Allah to bless me with riches. I do not wish to live in poverty."

The pious man prayed as requested and delivered the news to Fadl, cautioning him that his newfound wealth might not last more than two years.

Fadl responded, "Even if it lasts only two years, I only desire to experience wealth." Not long after, Fadl became incredibly rich.

However, he grew fearful that his wealth would soon vanish. He called upon his wife and shared his concerns, saying, "My dear wife, Allah has blessed us with wealth, but it is said to last only two years. How can we protect ourselves from poverty once the time comes?"

His wife replied, "As the head of the house, you should

propose a suggestion." Fadl pondered and suggested, "We could dig a hole and bury a substantial amount of money. That way, when Allah takes His wealth from us, we can continue to live in abundance."

His wife gently opposed the idea, saying, "Do you not think that would be unwise? If Allah wishes to take everything from us, He can send fire to burn the money buried beneath the earth. Instead, I suggest we build a house with four doors.

Through one door, we can offer clothes; through another, food; through the third, money; and through the fourth, assistance to those in need. So, when Allah makes us poor again, those we have helped will come to our aid in return."

Fadl considered her words and agreed, deeming it a good idea. They immediately set out to put this plan into action.

Word spread about how Fadl was generously helping others, and the pious man rejoiced upon hearing the news.

Time passed, and years went by—one, two, three, four, and even five—and Fadl remained exceedingly wealthy, even richer than before.

Intrigued, he decided to visit the pious man and inquire why his wealth had not diminished.

The pious man replied, "Allah tested you with wealth, and you have passed the test. As long as you remain generous, Allah will not take away your wealth. You were generous to the people, giving to others through four doors. However, Allah is the most bountiful."

Fun Fact:

The inspiring story "Allah the Bountiful" showcases the generosity and boundless blessings of Allah, a concept cherished in Islamic teachings.

In the Quran, Surah Al-Nahl (Chapter 16), Verse 18, it is stated:

"And if you should count the favors of Allah, you could not enumerate them. Indeed, Allah is Forgiving and Merciful."

This verse highlights the limitless abundance of Allah's blessings, which cannot be fully counted or comprehended. It encourages us to be grateful for the countless gifts bestowed upon us by the All-Merciful.

"Allah the Bountiful" beautifully reflects the essence of this Quranic verse, reminding of Allah's unending benevolence and the importance of expressing gratitude for His countless favours.

As you delve into this heartwarming tale, remember the profound wisdom of the Quran and let it inspire you to embrace a mindset of thankfulness and appreciation for the abundant blessings in your life.

LESSONS

1 We should learn to give to others from the blessings Allah has bestowed upon us.

2 When we give to others, Allah blesses us with more.

3 It is not good to be miserly or unwilling to share.

4 Allah is the most bountiful and generous.

New Words

Generous: Always willing to give or share.

Wealth: A large amount of money or possessions.

Poverty: The state of being poor.

Bounty: Abundance or a generous amount.

Unwise: Foolish or not sensible.

Pretended: To act as if something is true or behave in a certain way.

Beneath: Under or below.

Intrigued: Arose interest

QUESTIONS

01. What was the name of the poor man?

02. Who did the poor man ask to pray to Allah on his behalf?

03. For how many years did Allah promise to make the poor man rich?

04. Who suggested building a house with four doors?

05. Who is the most bountiful?

REMINDER

"Remember the blessings of generosity and helping others without expecting anything in return. Allah rewards those who selflessly assist those in need. Let kindness and compassion guide your actions."

★★★★★

Where is Your Proof?

Once upon a time, in a small town, there lived a widow who had two daughters. She was burdened by her poverty and the inability to provide for her children.

Determined to seek help, she decided to leave her town and journey to another place. After traveling a long distance, she arrived at a town inhabited by idolaters, with only one pious man residing there.

Unfamiliar with anyone in the town, she approached a woman she met along the way and pleaded, "Oh, kind woman, I am a poor widow with two daughters. I am in desperate need of help. Can you guide me to someone who can assist me in this town?"

The woman pointed towards a house and said, "Go to that house; it belongs to a pious man. I believe he can help you."

Following the woman's advice, the widow went to the

house of the pious man, leaving her daughters in the mosque owned by him. She explained her situation to the pious man, seeking his aid. However, he responded, "I am willing to help you, but first, where is the proof to support your claims?"

The widow was left speechless, filled with sadness, and departed from his presence. Not far away, she noticed another house and saw a man standing in front of it. Desperate, she approached him and shared her predicament. Although the man was an idolater, he chose to extend his help to the widow and her daughters. They began living with him, and their lives were filled with happiness.

One night, the pious man had a dream. He found himself in paradise, beholding a magnificent house. Curious, he inquired of the gatekeeper about the owner of the house. The gatekeeper responded, "This house belongs to the only pious man from your town." Filled with confidence, the pious man thought, "That must be me, for I am the only pious man from my town."

However, the gatekeeper challenged him by asking, "Where is your proof?" Startled, the pious man awoke from his dream, overwhelmed by fear. He remembered his encounter with the widow and realized that he needed to find her.

He discovered that the woman and her daughters were living with one of the idolaters. Upon reaching their dwelling, the pious man informed the idolater that the woman and her daughters were Muslims, and he wished for them to live with him since the idolater was not a Muslim.

However, the idolater refused to let them go, sharing his own story. He said, "Oh, pious one! I will not allow the widow and her daughters to live with you. When they arrived, I asked about their religion, and they stated they were Muslims.

However, because they were good-hearted individuals, I embraced their faith.

Two days later, I had a dream in which I entered the paradise garden and beheld a beautiful house. When

I inquired about the owner, the gatekeeper said it belonged to the only pious man in this town.

I believed it to be me, and I was granted entry as the rightful owner."

Upon hearing this, the pious man burst into tears, realizing that Allah had transformed the idolater into a pious man and favoured him due to his assistance to the widow and her daughters.

He deeply regretted demanding proof before offering his help, and returned home, weeping and seeking Allah's forgiveness.

KINDNESS JAR

Fill in acts of kindness you witness or receive from others.

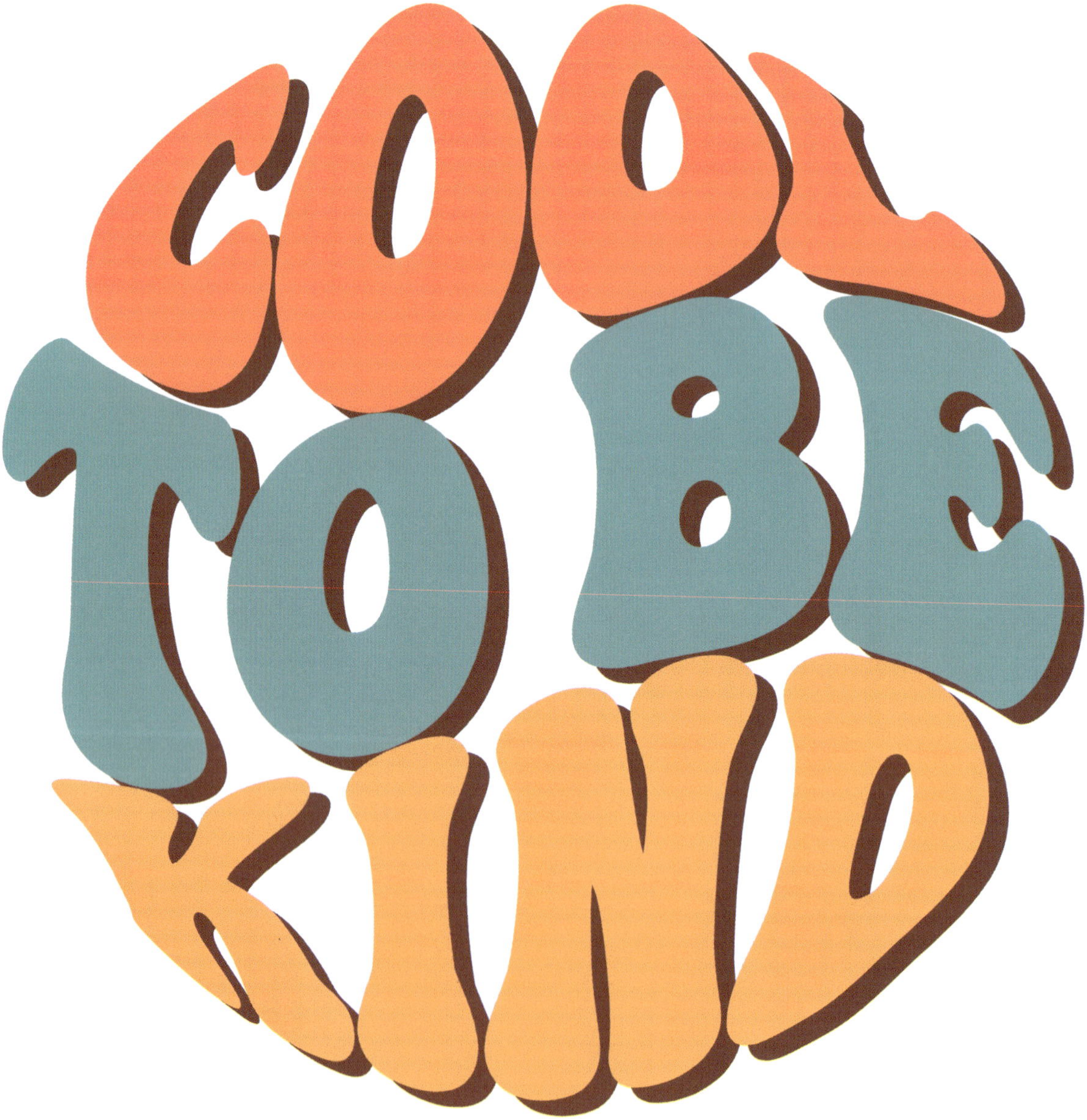
COOL
TO BE
KIND

LESSONS

1 We should extend help to others without requiring proof or reasons.

2 Allah loves those who perform good deeds.

3 It is important to show kindness to orphans and the needy, even if they are strangers.

New Words

Therein: Inside or within.

Favour: To show preference or support.

Idolaters: People who worship things other than Allah.

Regret: To feel sorry or remorseful.

Widow: A woman whose husband has passed away and has not remarried.

Render: To give or provide.

Proof: Evidence or something to support a claim.

Paradise: The place where virtuous people will reside after death.

QUESTIONS

01. How many daughters did the widow in the story have?

02. Who is a widow?

03. Whom did the gatekeeper allow to enter the house?

REMINDER

"Remember the blessings of generosity and helping others without expecting anything in return. Allah rewards those who selflessly assist those in need. Let kindness and compassion guide your actions."

★★★★★

GENEROSITY AND TRUST IN ALLAH NEW WORDS PUZZLE

Words can be found in any direction (including diagonals) and can overlap each other. Use the word bank below.

```
F I X O Z U U H U K O I B P Y C D B I T
O T C R E Q D Q N J Q O V W R S P N N F
O R H U G F T K Z U K S P U G K L M X
H D S E U O Z X N N R U O V A F U P Q T
U E L V R U W K T W F P W N N U I T M R
B Q G J F E S Y E F L Z P P V O P O R E
G L B L Z M I M R V A A W M R B O U S G
I I P R L L N G E R N U G V M V G V R
M U H N W A H W M A N N B I K Z E B T E
N J A C L H M I D U W D N Q G T R X O T
I J V C T B J I E I B P E K H T T M U T
M I W E O U S I S B E S M R M B Y B X O
W D A E C E C E W N N P U F C A Y O E I
U O Z O A I P H F D E O R O P E I T W Q
S L D M B L W A F K A T A O R H G N H O
A A T I M W T E X E T U E V O E B K Y X
Z T Q D W R K H O N H X Z N S F N X F N
B E P W F X P E I V W W D D L Q C E L K
X R D R S R L Z Y R G Y V N I W A U G E
Z S D B H U S Y H Q V Q W J M E H B Y F
```

Word Bank

1. THEREIN
2. POVERTY
3. BOUNTY
4. WINDOW
5. WEALTH
6. RENDER
7. UNWISE
8. REGRET
9. PROOF
10. FAVOUR
11. PARADISE
12. BENEATH
13. IDOLATORS
14. GENEROUS

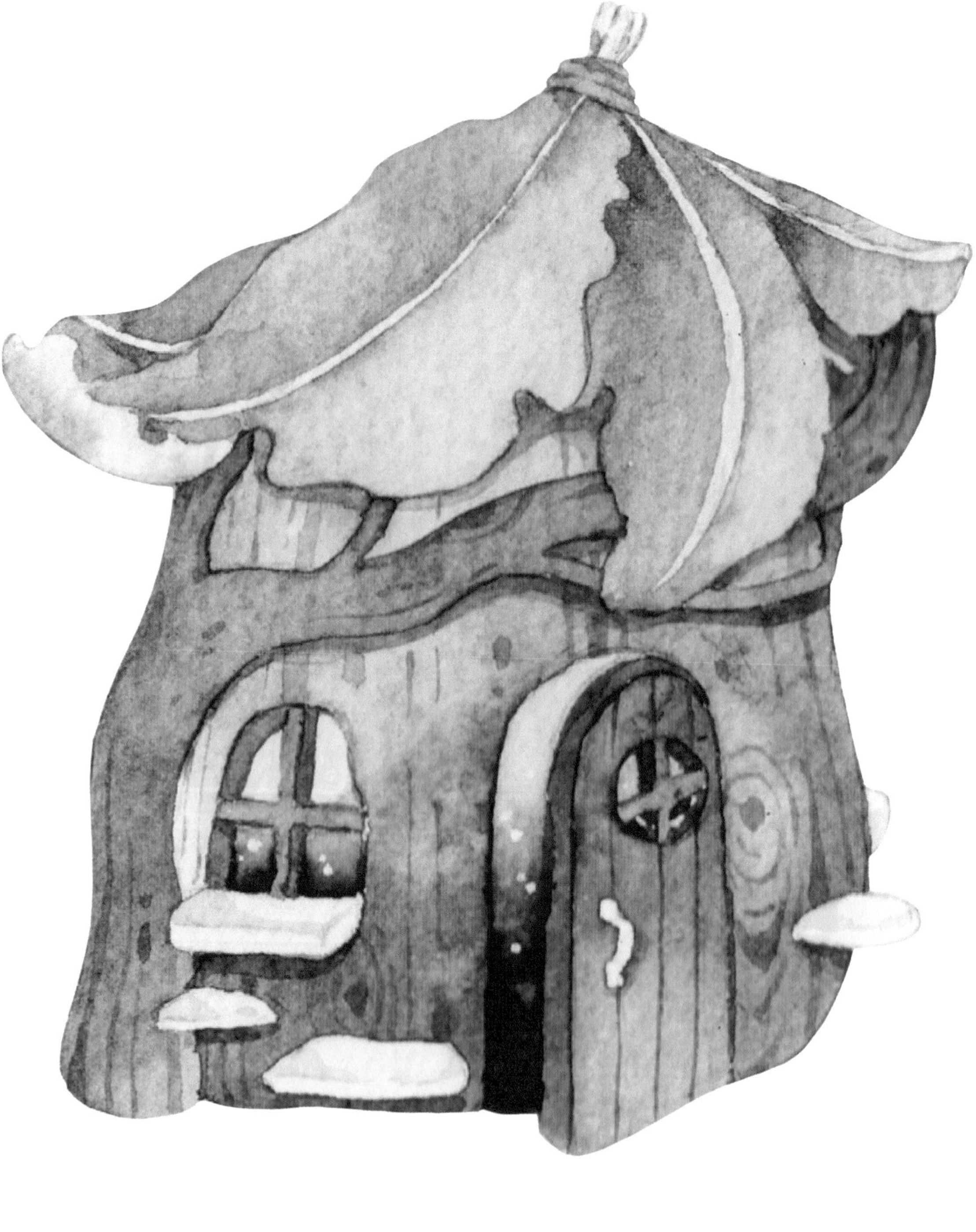

Consequences of Actions

EQUALITY AND JUSTICE

During the lifetime of the Holy Prophet Muhammad ﷺ, there lived a woman named Fatima Al-Makhzumi, belonging to a respected and noble family.

Unfortunately, Fatima was involved in a theft that warranted the punishment of having her hand cut off.

However, due to her high social status, the people from her tribe believed that such a judgment should not apply to someone of her class.

They felt that people from privileged backgrounds should be treated differently from the commoners.

To convince the Prophet ﷺ about this, they decided to send Usama, the son of Zayd (the adopted son of the Holy Prophet Muhammad ﷺ).

Usama approached the Prophet ﷺ and said, "Oh Prophet of Allah, have you heard about Fatima from the tribe of Makhzumi, who shares the same name as your daughter? She has been accused of theft. She comes from a noble tribe, and no one from her tribe has ever faced punishment before. Please release her without penalty."

The Prophet ﷺ became angry upon hearing this and replied, "Oh Usama, I hold great affection for you, but consider what you are asking me. Are you suggesting that I should not adhere to the commandments of Allah?"

Realizing his mistake, Usama felt remorseful and begged for forgiveness.

The Prophet ﷺ then gathered everyone together and proclaimed, "In the era before Islam, there was injustice, but now that Islam has arrived, justice must prevail, and everyone should be treated equally.

By Allah, in whose hands my life rests, if it were my own daughter, Fatima, I would do the same."

FUN FACT:

In this story, we learn that even during the time of the Prophet Muhammad ﷺ, the importance of equality and justice was emphasized.

When a woman named Fatima from a noble family was accused of theft, some people wanted her to be treated differently because of her status.

However, the Prophet ﷺ knew that fairness and justice should apply to everyone, no matter their background or social class. He ﷺ made it clear that in Islam, everyone should be treated equally, and no one should be above the law.

This story teaches us that treating everyone fairly and justly is essential, no matter who they are. It reminds us that in the eyes of justice, everyone is equal, and no one should be favored or treated differently because of their status or name.

LESSONS

1 Islam promotes and upholds the principles of justice.

2 In the sight of Allah, everyone is equal regardless of their social status.

3 Every good leader should follow the example of the Holy Prophet in rendering fair judgments.

4 The Holy Prophet Muhammad (peace and blessings of Allah be upon him) was a just and righteous leader.

New Words

Injustice: The absence or violation of justice.

Justice: The correct application of law or fairness.

Respectable: Holding a position of honor or esteem.

Theft: The act of stealing.

Noble: Having high social rank or status.

Convince: To persuade or make someone believe.

Judgment: A decision made in a legal context.

QUESTIONS

01. What was the name of the thief?

02. She belonged to the tribe of _____.

03. Who was sent to plead with the Prophet?

04. According to the story, Islam preaches

REMINDER

"Stand up for justice and treat everyone equally. Status and background should not determine how we are treated or judge others. Uphold fairness and follow in the footsteps of the Prophet Muhammad (Peace and blessings of Allah be upon him)."

★★★★★

THE THREE YOUNG MEN

On a cold and windy day, three young men set out on a journey. However, as they continued, the wind grew stronger and a thunderstorm approached.

Seeking shelter, they decided to take refuge in a cave. To their surprise, as soon as they entered the cave, a strong gust of wind rolled a large rock to block the entrance. They waited, hoping the storm would pass and they could continue their journey.

But when they tried to leave, they discovered that the rock was too heavy for them to move.

Realizing their predicament, they turned to supplication and sought the help of Allah.

One after the other, they made heartfelt prayers. The first young man prayed to Allah, mentioning how he prioritizes caring for his aging parents, even putting their needs before his own family's. He recalled an incident where he patiently waited for his sleeping parents to wake up before giving them milk to drink.

He asked Allah to move the rock, and miraculously, it shifted away from the entrance. However, the opening was still too narrow for them to pass through.

The second young man stepped forward and pleaded with Allah, sharing an incident where he was tempted to take advantage of his cousin's vulnerability in exchange for lending her money. However, her words of reminding him to fear Allah stopped him from committing the wrongdoing.

He prayed to Allah, asking for the rock to be moved, and once again, it shifted, but the space remained insufficient.

Finally, the third young man offered his supplication. He spoke of a time when he had employed workers and paid them their wages. However, one worker left before collecting his payment.

Unable to find him, the young man invested the worker's money in cattle rearing, which eventually grew into a large herd. When the worker returned years later, the young man handed over the entire herd, leaving nothing for himself.

He implored Allah to move the rock, and this time, it moved enough to create a wide passage for all of them to exit the cave.

Filled with gratitude, the three young men thanked Allah for His mercy and realized the greatness of His rewards for their good deeds when done solely for His sake.

Fun Facts:

In the amazing story of "The Three Young Men," three brave friends got stuck in a cave because of a big rock that blocked the entrance. But they didn't give up! They knew Allah could help them.

Each friend told Allah about the good things they did. One friend told Allah how he always took care of his old parents, even before himself. Another friend shared how he resisted a temptation to do something wrong and listened to his cousin's good advice. The last friend talked about being honest and giving back money to someone, even when it was hard.

Guess what happened? Because they were sincere and good in their hearts, Allah heard them and moved the rock a little bit. When they called upon Allah again, He moved the rock more! Finally, they could come out of the cave, safe and happy.

This story teaches us that when we are kind, truthful, and do good things for Allah's sake, He helps us too. We should always call upon Allah, be sincere, and know that He is there for us. Allah is the Most Merciful and rewards us for doing good things with a pure heart. How wonderful is that!

LESSONS

1 Allah values and rewards those who care for their parents.

2 It is essential to fear Allah and abstain from actions that go against His teachings.

3 Taking what does not belong to us is forbidden; we should always strive for honesty and integrity.

4 Whenever we face difficulties, we should turn to Allah for help through supplication and prayer.

5 Our good deeds, performed sincerely for the sake of Allah, serve as a means of seeking His assistance and blessings.

New Words

Struck: Touched or deeply affected.

Invest: To use money for a business or financial purpose.

Wage: Payment for work or labour.

Supplicate: To pray or make a heartfelt request.

Cave: A hollow space or cavity in the rock.

Embarked: Started or began.

QUESTIONS

01. According to the story, how many travellers were there?

02. How did Allah reward the men for their good deeds?

03. State four lessons you have learned from the story.

REMINDER

"Perseverance and faith can overcome challenges. When faced with difficulties, turn to Allah and seek His guidance. Remember the power of supplication and trust in Allah's mercy. Together, we can conquer obstacles and find a way forward."

★★★★★

CONSEQUENCES OF ACTIONS NEW WORDS PUZZLE

Words can be found in any direction (including diagonals) and can overlap each other. Use the word bank below.

```
S E C I T S U J N I A H E J B K Z E F B
G M V Z O A S U P P L I C A T E G N M X
I D M A V N G Y G P L A Q X Y A E C S J
R G O T C V N T U R Q Y E D F U U C E S
C V D Q Q E Y K H E L B A T C E P S E R
R N T Y E P U S S A L C S U B M E B I E
A M T R C B T I E L I B B T M C E D D H
D W U Y N S T A Y Z E R O E R X O A D Y
J D F A E R Q H A S I L M N S U U F J K
S G P V P B L K E W V L X J O M C D X K
E U N W S O H S E F N V F V C Q W K Y F
U I Y C Q I Z H Y T T V N H B P M O C N
H F Y I W V V K Z Q Z T N E M G D U J E
M T F Q W A H K M R J Q O G G B Q U C L
X D Y X Y K W S L Y T I B R E O P N A B
D N A S E K A S I I R B H G X L I W A J
G Y S X C B G E M B A R K E D V A Z X D
H E P K S X E M O B G X T D N U Y C T B
K R E J U S T I C E O M K O S G C K L E
D F M P H X W Q F Q L C C P K U N M V G
```

Word Bank

1. INJUSTICE
2. INVEST
3. THEFT
4. STRUCK
5. WAGE
6. EMBARKED
7. CONVINCE
8. CAVE
9. RESPECTABLE
10. NOBLE
11. JUSTICE
12. JUDGMENT
13. SUPPLICATE

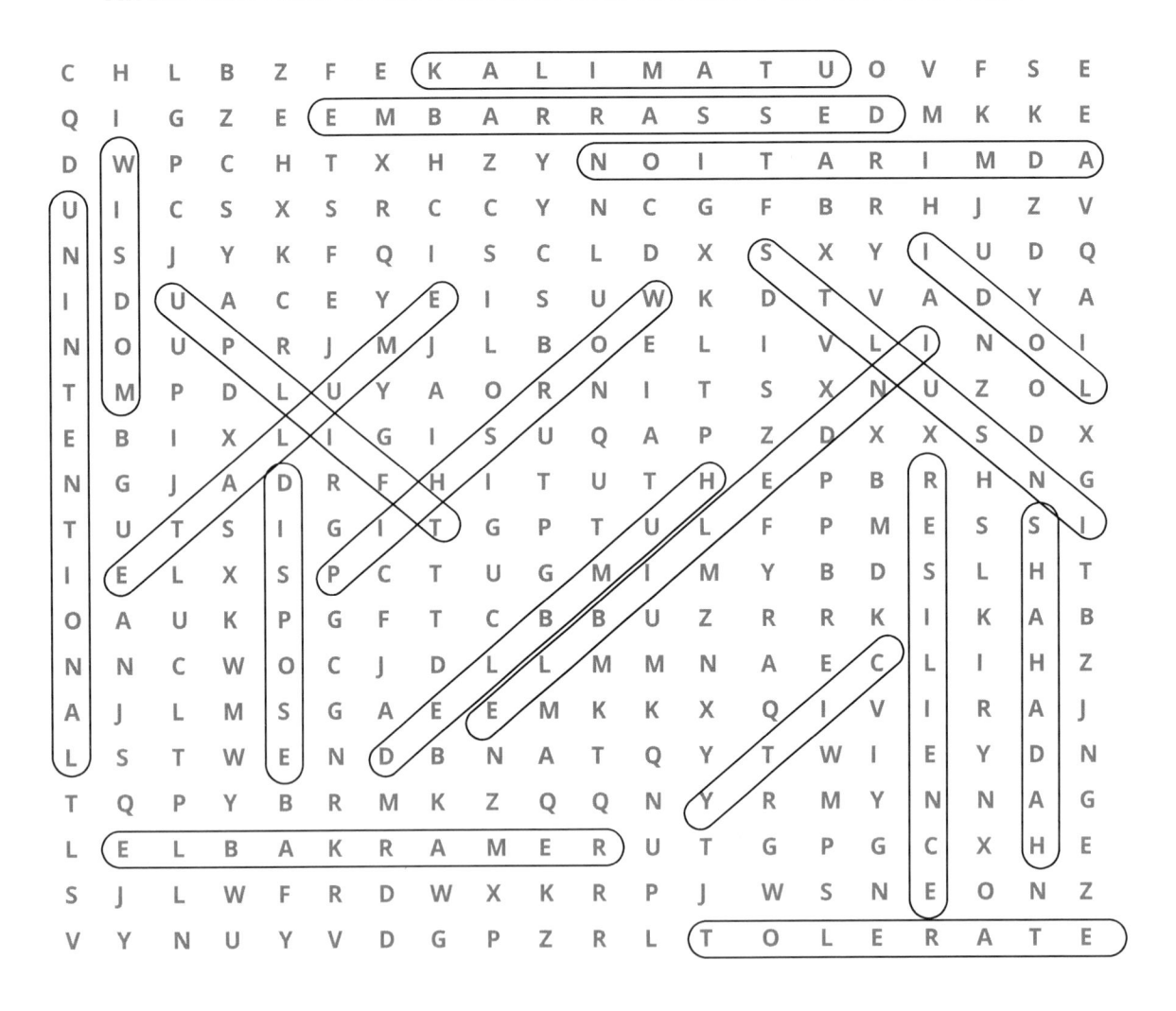

KINDNESS AND COMPASSION NEW WORDS PUZZLE - ANSWER

C	H	L	B	Z	F	E	K	A	L	I	M	A	T	U	O	V	F	S	E
Q	I	G	Z	E	E	M	B	A	R	R	A	S	S	E	D	M	K	K	E
D	W	P	C	H	T	X	H	Z	Y	N	O	I	T	A	R	I	M	D	A
U	I	C	S	X	S	R	C	C	Y	N	C	G	F	B	R	H	J	Z	V
N	S	J	Y	K	F	Q	I	S	C	L	D	X	S	X	Y	I	U	D	Q
I	D	U	A	C	E	Y	E	I	S	U	W	K	D	T	V	A	D	Y	A
N	O	U	P	R	J	M	J	L	B	O	E	L	I	V	L	I	N	O	I
T	M	P	D	L	U	Y	A	O	R	N	I	T	S	X	N	U	Z	O	L
E	B	I	X	L	I	G	I	S	U	Q	A	P	Z	D	X	X	S	D	X
N	G	J	A	D	R	F	H	I	T	U	T	H	E	P	B	R	H	N	G
T	U	T	S	I	G	I	T	G	P	T	U	L	F	P	M	E	S	S	I
I	E	L	X	S	P	C	T	U	G	M	I	M	Y	B	D	S	L	H	T
O	A	U	K	P	G	F	T	C	B	B	U	Z	R	R	K	I	K	A	B
N	N	C	W	O	C	J	D	L	L	M	M	N	A	E	C	L	I	H	Z
A	J	L	M	S	G	A	E	E	M	K	K	X	Q	I	V	I	R	A	J
L	S	T	W	E	N	D	B	N	A	T	Q	Y	T	W	I	E	Y	D	N
T	Q	P	Y	B	R	M	K	Z	Q	Q	N	Y	R	M	Y	N	N	A	G
L	E	L	B	A	K	R	A	M	E	R	U	T	G	P	G	C	X	H	E
S	J	L	W	F	R	D	W	X	K	R	P	J	W	S	N	E	O	N	Z
V	Y	N	U	Y	V	D	G	P	Z	R	L	T	O	L	E	R	A	T	E

86

LEARNING THE HARD WAY NEW WORDS PUZZLE - ANSWER

B	O	K	A	N	I	V	X	C	S	R	N	H	Y	S	R	G	K	U	H
N	A	D	D	O	W	Y	P	O	T	J	X	S	X	A	N	P	N	C	D
O	M	H	E	I	R	B	D	N	R	F	X	N	F	V	Y	F	D	O	C
I	I	H	T	S	E	L	P	S	U	J	X	G	E	L	O	S	N	N	J
T	S	I	E	S	C	H	S	U	C	H	V	T	H	R	R	R	R	S	F
C	T	W	S	I	O	C	X	M	K	D	J	S	T	E	T	Z	I	I	B
U	A	F	I	O	G	L	W	E	Y	Q	I	U	G	J	T	G	Y	D	H
R	K	F	M	R	N	G	T	D	N	L	N	A	K	Y	D	F	X	E	O
T	E	P	N	E	I	F	K	B	Y	A	L	J	I	W	S	R	J	R	S
S	N	F	E	P	T	Y	R	T	T	L	G	O	M	U	H	U	F	A	P
N	L	E	D	Q	I	W	S	E	I	B	E	K	I	I	S	Q	D	T	I
I	Y	G	K	Q	O	L	L	V	K	A	B	F	J	T	Y	F	E	E	T
V	P	D	Q	B	N	Y	H	L	W	Y	S	M	U	Q	L	D	D	N	A
H	U	R	R	I	E	D	L	Y	A	H	R	B	X	E	N	N	N	T	L
J	O	H	K	O	D	X	O	R	Y	M	B	R	I	Q	E	E	E	D	I
U	I	W	V	P	U	P	A	I	T	O	E	P	A	F	D	S	S	Y	Z
A	V	D	V	C	X	P	Z	B	R	K	L	N	Q	M	D	P	E	R	E
V	C	G	E	B	M	J	V	N	J	J	A	T	T	U	U	R	R	J	D
V	Q	K	L	A	E	Y	O	Y	C	I	K	E	V	E	S	O	P	O	H
S	E	C	N	E	U	Q	E	S	N	O	C	Y	D	X	D	C	U	E	M

87

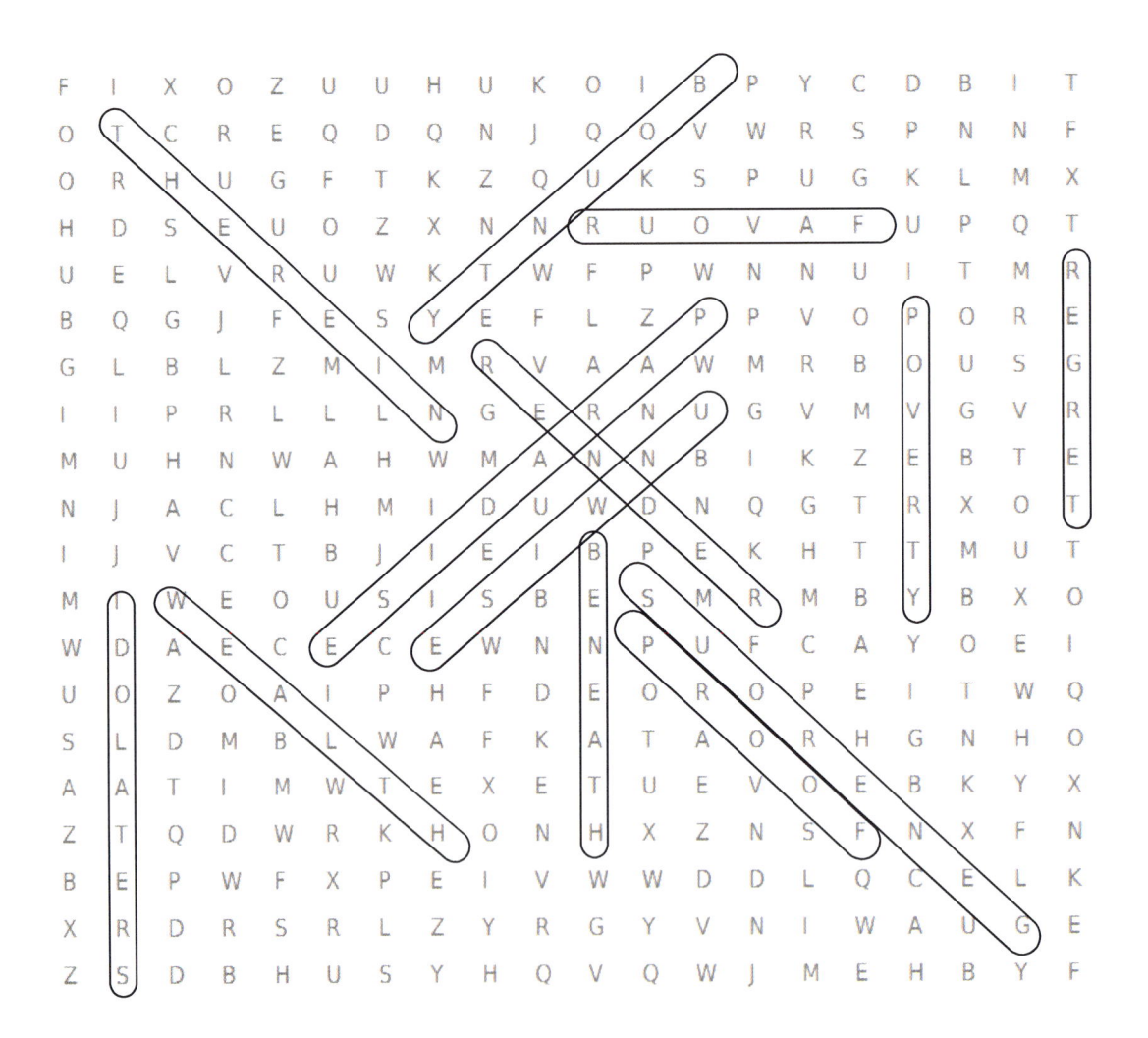

GENEROSITY AND TRUST IN ALLAH NEW WORDS PUZZLE - ANSWER

CONSEQUENCES OF ACTIONS NEW WORDS PUZZLE - ANSWER

```
S E C I T S U J N I A H E J B K Z E F B
G M V Z O A S U P P L I C A T E G N M X
I D M A V N G Y G P L A Q X Y A E C S J
R G O T C V N T U R Q Y E D F U U C E S
C V D Q Q E Y K H E L B A T C E P S E R
R N T Y E P U S S A L C S U B M E B I E
A M T R C B T I E L I B B T M C E D D H
D W U Y N S T A Y Z E R O E R X O A D Y
J D F A E R Q H A S I L M N S U U F J K
S G P V P B L K E W V L X J O M C D X K
E U N W S O H S E F N V F V C Q W K Y F
U I Y C Q I Z H Y T T V N H B P M O C N
H F Y I W V V K Z Q Z T N E M G D U J E
M T F Q W A H K M R J Q O G G B Q U C L
X D Y X Y K W S L Y T I B R E O P N A B
D N A S E K A S I I R B H G X L I W A J
G Y S X C B G E M B A R K E D V A Z X D
H E P K S X E M O B G X T D N U Y C T B
K R E J U S T I C E O M K O S G C K L E
D F M P H X W Q F Q L C C P K U N M V G
```

89

CONCLUSION

Dear readers,

As we come to the end of our journey through these captivating stories, it is important to reflect on the values and lessons we have learned. Each tale has carried its own unique message, touching our hearts and minds in profound ways. Now, let us gather these precious lessons and weave them into the fabric of our lives.

The stories we have encountered remind us of the timeless virtues that shape our character: kindness, courage, honesty, perseverance, and empathy. These values serve as guiding lights, illuminating the path we tread in our daily lives. They encourage us to treat others with respect, to stand up for what is right, and to embrace diversity and understanding.

But stories alone are not enough. It is in the application of these lessons that their true power is revealed. We must strive to embody these values in our actions and decisions, in our interactions with friends and family, and in the choices we make at school or in our communities. By living these lessons, we become agents of positive change, spreading ripples of compassion and goodness wherever we go.

Remember that even the smallest actions can have a tremendous impact. A kind word or a helping hand can brighten someone's day. An act of courage can inspire others to find their own strength. Honesty and integrity can build trust and foster deeper connections. Perseverance can unlock our true potential, leading to personal growth and achievement. And empathy can bridge divides, fostering understanding and harmony in our world.

Never underestimate the power you hold within you. Your actions matter, and your choices shape the world around you. As you embark on this beautiful journey called life, carry these values close to your heart and let them guide your every step. Let the stories you have read be a constant reminder of the difference you can make and the positive impact you can have on the lives of others.

May you always find joy in the pages of a book, where stories come alive and imagination knows no bounds. And may the lessons you have learned from these stories inspire you to become the heroes and heroines of your own stories, making the world a brighter and more compassionate place for all.

With warmest wishes,

Kafeelah Adenekan

Printed in Great Britain
by Amazon